MW01534308

LEOPARD'S COAT

Written by John Hare
Illustrated by Eva Gundersen

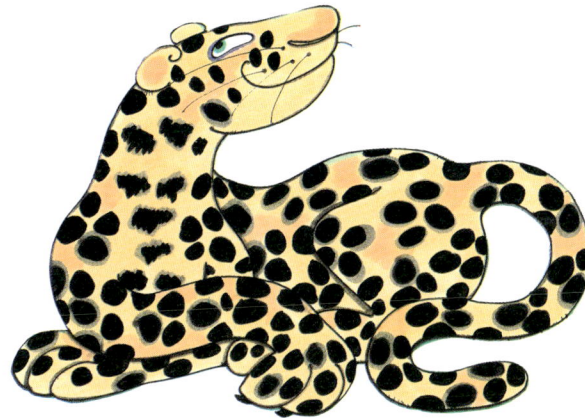

Hodder & Stoughton
Headway

Leopard was born with a very smart coat.

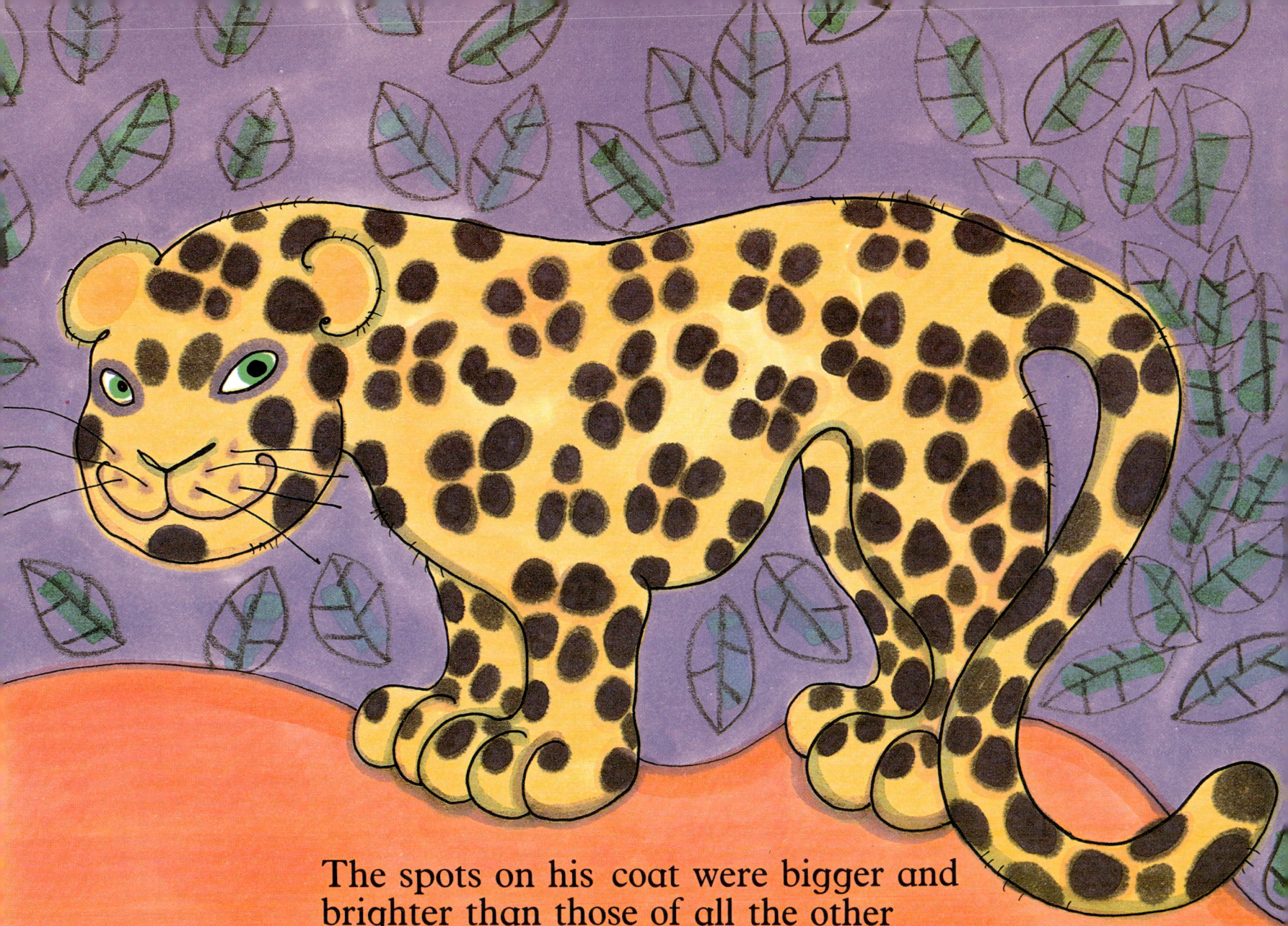

The spots on his coat were bigger and
brighter than those of all the other
leopards in the bush.

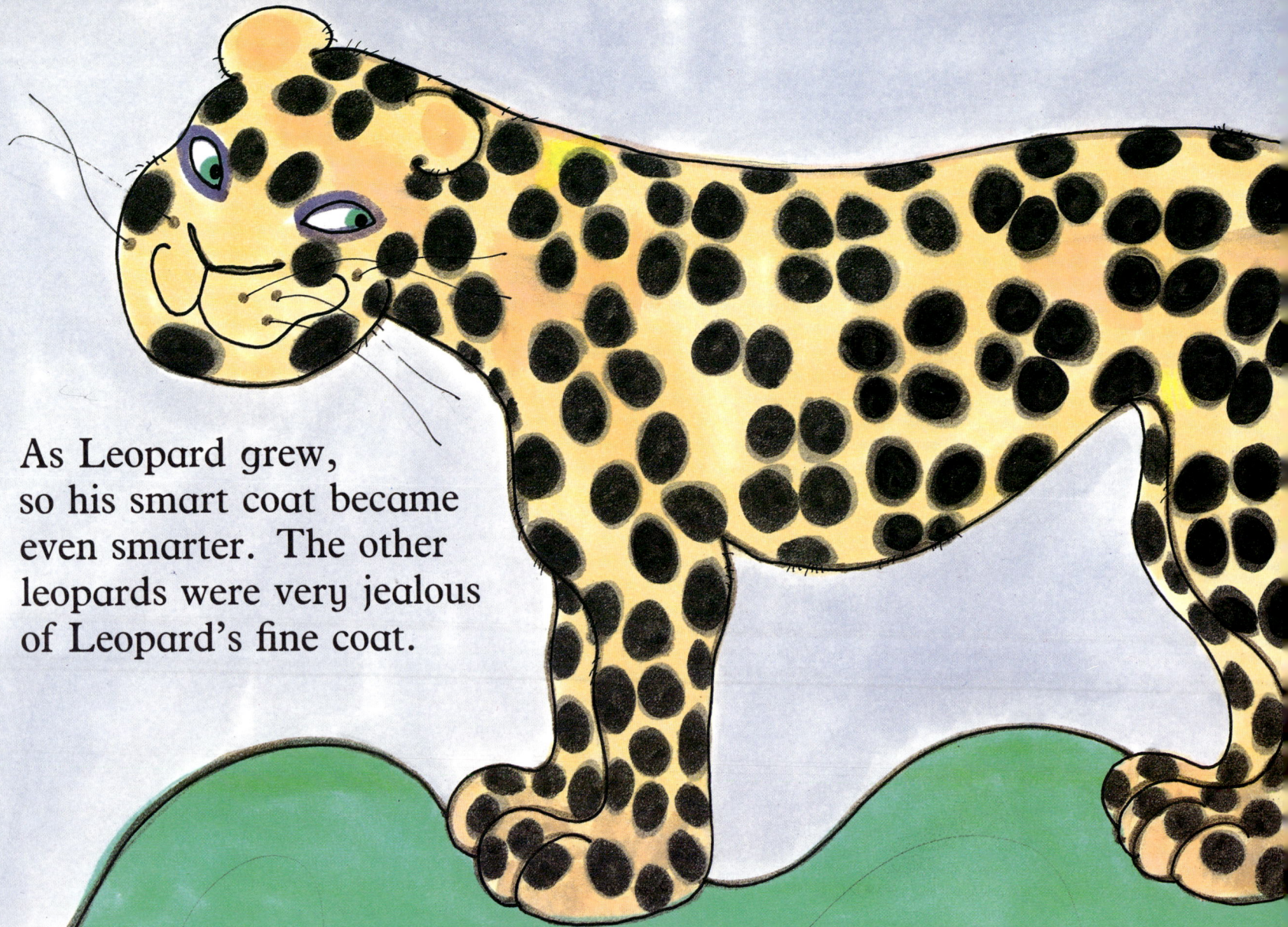

As Leopard grew,
so his smart coat became
even smarter. The other
leopards were very jealous
of Leopard's fine coat.

One day, they decided to teach Leopard a lesson. They invited Leopard to play with them beside a newly-formed watering hole. The water was cool and clear and they knew that Leopard would want to stand in it and admire his beautiful coat.

However, one side of the watering hole was surrounded by dark, sticky mud. The other leopards persuaded Leopard to enter the water. He strutted down to the water's edge to admire himself and immediately sank into the mud.

The other leopards laughed at Leopard and ignored his cries for help. How they laughed to see his smart coat all black and dirty. 'That will teach you to show off in front of us,' they cried.

Suddenly, a rifle shot rang out. All the leopards scattered and ran off into the thick bush. A hunter had come to try to kill them so that he could take away their coats and sell them.

Poor Leopard struggled
desperately to escape but only
succeeded in sinking even
deeper into the mud.

When the hunter saw that Leopard was stuck in the mud he raised his rifle to shoot him. But when he saw how dirty Leopard's coat was, he decided that it would not be worth any money so he lowered his rifle and went away.

Vultures started to circle over Leopard. They looked down at him with their beady eyes wondering how much longer it would be before Leopard finally died and they could eat him up.

It grew dark. Leopard became weaker and weaker. He stopped struggling to try to free himself for he felt certain that he was going to die.

Elephant had had a long tiring day. He was very thirsty and although it was late he decided to go down to the watering hole for a drink.

When Elephant reached
the watering hole he saw
Leopard. He wrapped
his great trunk around
Leopard and pulled him
out of the mud.

'This has happened because you are too proud,' said Elephant as he blew water over Leopard to help him to clean his coat. 'I have learned my lesson,' Leopard replied. 'I will never be proud of my coat again.'

And yet, thought Leopard, afterwards when he was dry and safe, if my coat had not been dirty I would have been shot.

I wonder if people really need to kill me for my coat.

I don't think so – DO YOU?

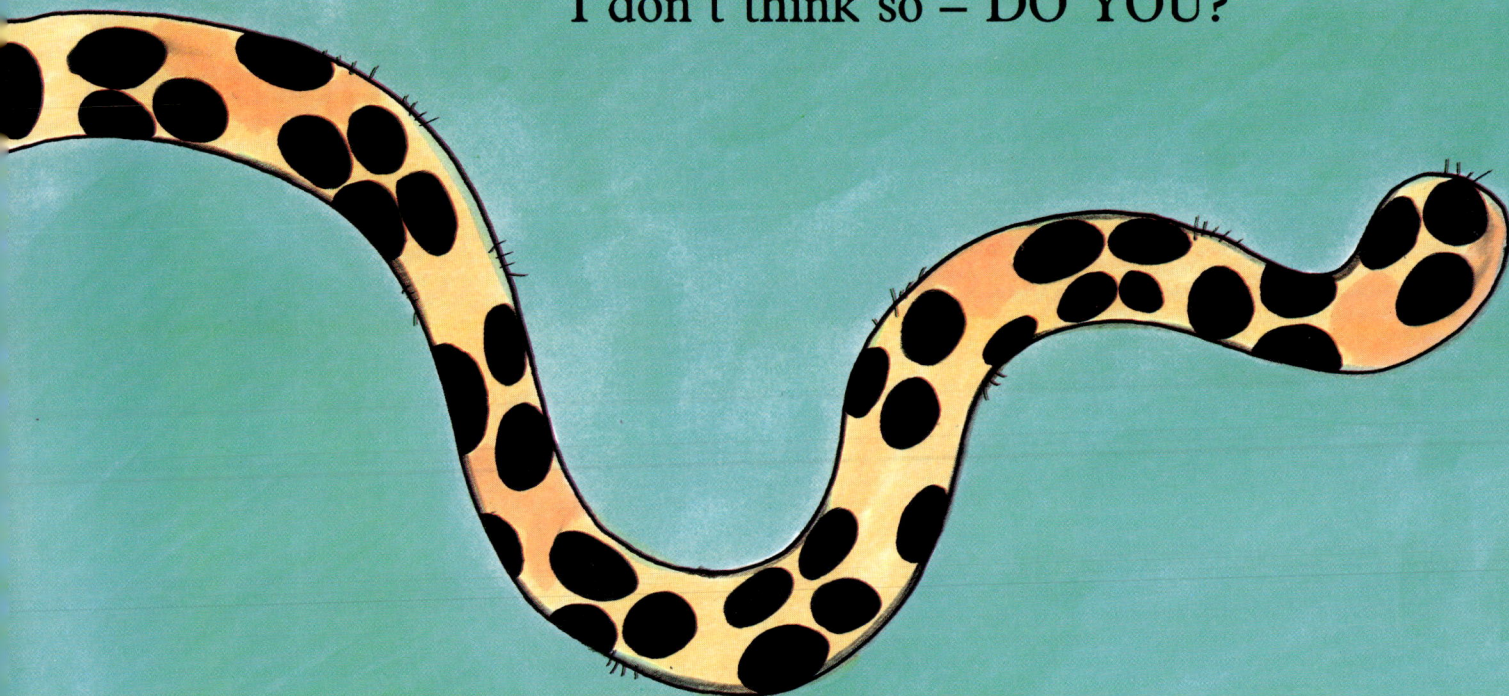

Note to parents from WWF:

We hope your child enjoys reading this book and learning about nature.

WWF has worked since 1961 to save not only animals, such as those in this book, but also the forests and wetlands and other habitats in which they live.

Your local WWF office can provide you with additional ways to inform your children about nature.

for: Charlotte, Hetta and Emily

British Library Cataloguing in Publication Data

Hare, John
1, Leopard's Coat
I. Title. II. Gundersen, Eva
8231. 914 (J)

ISBN 0-340-50518-4

First published 1989

Photoset in Great Britain by Rowland Phototypesetting Limited, Bury St Edmunds, Suffolk.
Printed in Great Britain for Hodder and Stoughton Educational, a division of Hodder and Stoughton Limited, Mill Road, Dunton Green, Sevenoaks, Kent by Colorcraft Limited.